Rebecca Faulkner | **How to get ahead in**

Healthcare

www.raintreepublishers.co.uk

Visit our website to find out more information about **Raintree** books.

To order:
☎ Phone 44 (0) 1865 888113
📄 Send a fax to 44 (0) 1865 314091
💻 Visit the Raintree bookshop at **www.raintreepublishers.co.uk**
to browse our catalogue and order online.

First published in Great Britain by Raintree,
Halley Court, Jordan Hill, Oxford OX2 8EJ,
part of Harcourt Education.
Raintree is a registered trademark of
Harcourt Education Ltd.

Editorial: Melanie Waldron and Lucy Beevor
Design: David Poole and Calcium
Illustrations: Geoff Ward
Picture Research: Melissa Allison
and Fiona Orbell
Production: Huseyin Sami

Originated by Chroma Graphics
Printed and bound in China by
South China Printing Company

10 digit ISBN 1 406 20444 7
13 digit ISBN 978 1 406 20444 5

11 10 09 08 07
10 9 8 7 6 5 4 3 2 1

British Library Cataloguing in Publication Data
Faulkner, Rebecca
Healthcare. – (How to get ahead in)
362.1'02341
A full catalogue record for this book is available
from the British Library.

Acknowledgements
The publishers would like to thank the following
for permission to reproduce photographs: Alamy
pp. 19 (Frances Roberts), 25 (OnRequest
Images, Inc), 21 (Paul Glendell), 11, 50
(Photofusion Picture Library), 26 (Thinkstock);
Corbis pp. 4 (Bernado Bucci), 5 (Ed Bock), 24
(George Shelley), 9 (Randy Duchaine), 14 (Robert
Wallis), 6, 7, 32 (Royalty-Free), 15 (zefa/C. Lyttle);
Education Photos pp. 34, 48 (Lynd Westmore);
Getty Images pp. 13 (Image Bank), 27
(Photodisc), 22 (Stone); Photofusion Picture
Library pp. 17, 38 (Jacky Chapman), 8 (Paula
Solloway), 36 (Vehbi Koca); reportdigital.co.uk
pp. 46 (Duncan Phillips), 20 (Jess Hurd);
Wellcome Trust Medical Photo Library pp. 10,
29, p. 40 (Ilianski).

Cover photograph of stethoscopes reproduced
with permission of Getty Images/Photographer's
Choice.

The publishers would like to thank Gillian Milner
for her assistance in the preparation of this
book.

Contents

Words appearing in the text in bold, **like this**, are explained in the glossary.

Acareer in healthcare – saving lives, curing illnesses, and improving the quality of people's lives – sounds like the perfect job, doesn't it? But is this really what it involves? Finding all the information to help you decide if this is the career for you can be difficult. That is where this book comes in. It will give you an introduction to what the healthcare industry is and what sorts of jobs it offers, and help you work out if you would like to work in this industry. It will also show you that there is a lot more to the healthcare industry than just caring for people who are ill.

It is very important to find the career that suits you so that you will be happy in your job. To find the right career needs a lot of careful thought and planning. This book aims to help you make the right decision.

YOUR CAREER ADVISOR

This book cannot tell you everything about the healthcare industry – it can only give you an introduction. You can get more advice from your careers advisor at school. He or she will be able to help you choose the right career for you.

below: *There are many different roles in the healthcare industry, each playing a vital part in the lives of millions of people.*

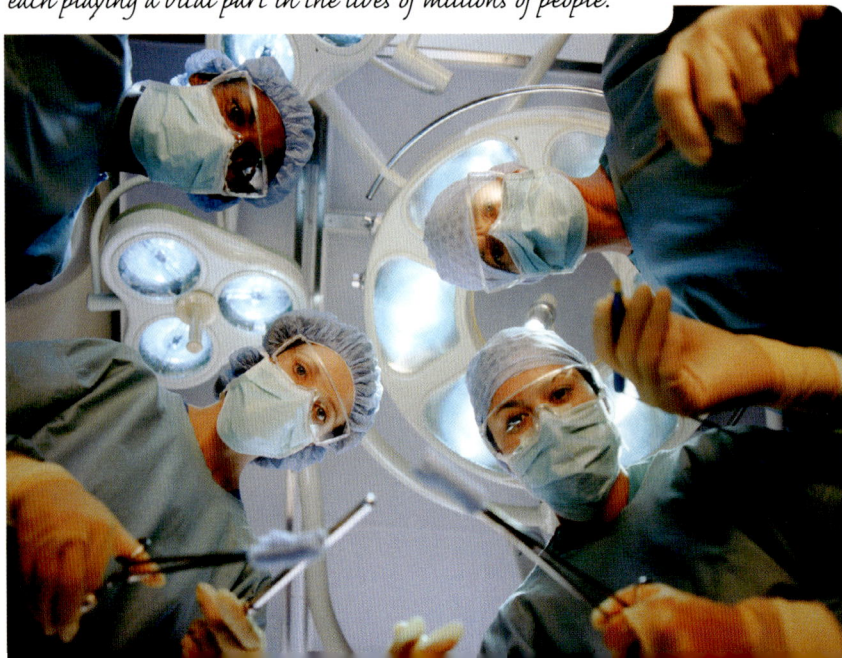

What do you imagine when you think of healthcare? Do you picture a scene from *ER* or *Casualty*? Maybe a heart surgeon in the operating theatre or a **paramedic** rushing a patient from an ambulance to the hospital? These are just two of many different types of careers in the healthcare industry.

Most hospitals are run by the **National Health Service** (NHS) and it employs over 1 million people in the UK. However, this is not your only option for employment, there are also private hospitals, clinics, and nursing homes, as well as drug companies and laboratories where many healthcare jobs can be found.

A career in healthcare can be challenging, exciting, and rewarding. It will also be very hard work. In many areas of the healthcare industry there is a shortage of workers. In some parts of the UK doctors and nurses are in very high demand. However, in other parts of the UK it is more difficult to get a job as staffing levels are high. If you are prepared to work hard, however, you will find the right job for you.

THE NHS

The NHS provides healthcare for everyone in the UK, from the accident and emergency departments in hospitals, to long-term healthcare, clinics, and dentistry.

right: *It takes a huge amount of research and testing to produce the vast numbers of medical drugs that are available.*

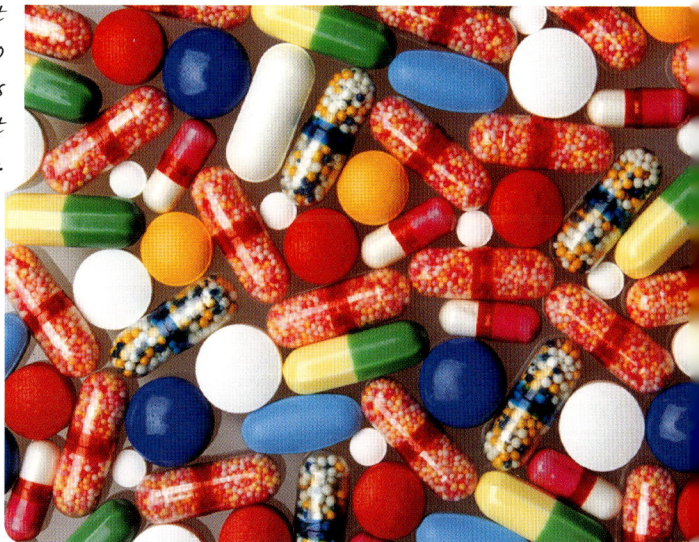

Chapter 1

What is the healthcare industry?

Before we go any further, let's think clearly about what healthcare actually is. Healthcare is all about helping people who are ill, injured, or in need of support in their daily lives. This may be caring for people in hospital, doing research to find new or improved treatments for illnesses, educating people about good health, or helping people overcome their problems through **counselling** and support.

The healthcare industry

The healthcare industry provides the facilities, products, and services to help people who are ill. You may have come into contact with people who work in the healthcare industry – for example, your family doctor – but what do you think it would be like to actually work in this industry?

below: *Training and studying are essential for many healthcare jobs.*

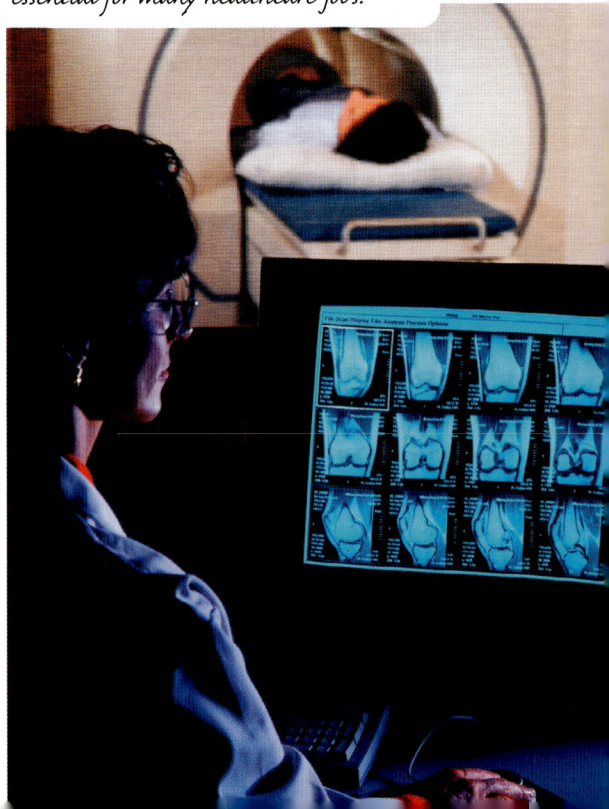

TWO MAIN AREAS

The healthcare industry can be divided into two main areas: primary healthcare and secondary healthcare.

◎ Primary healthcare is the type of healthcare you are more likely to be familiar with. This is the healthcare provided by your family doctor, dentist, **optician**, and chemist.

◎ Secondary healthcare is the care provided by ambulance drivers, nurses, and doctors if you have to go into hospital.

There is a whole range of careers within primary and secondary healthcare. The main sectors of the healthcare industry are described below. As you read through, think about whether one or more sectors appeal to you more than the others.

Get ahead!

Find out and list all the places a doctor can work. You will need to think much further afield than NHS hospitals.

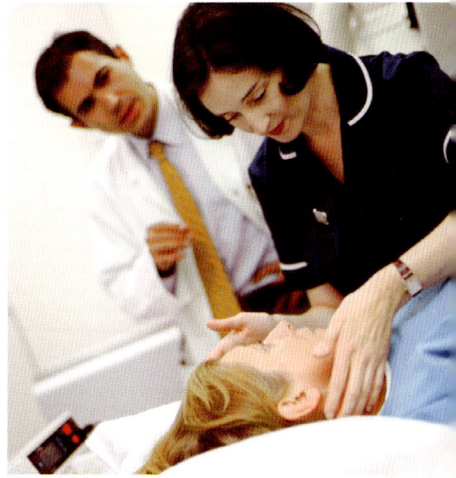

Doctors

Do you want a challenging career with a chance to make a difference? As a doctor your job will include diagnosing ill health, treating illnesses, and understanding the reasons why people become ill.

There are many branches of medicine offering a variety of career opportunities for doctors. Most hospital doctors are employed by the National Health Service (NHS), but most **general practitioners** (GPs) are self-employed partners in a practice and work in the community. **Locum** doctors provide cover for doctors who are ill or on holiday.

above: *Both doctors and nurses work in hospitals to care for patients.*

As well as working for the NHS, there are also opportunities for doctors to work in private hospitals and clinics. Wherever they practise, all doctors must be registered with the **General Medical Council** (GMC).

A WIDE CHOICE OF CAREERS

There are many specialist careers a doctor can follow such as:
- **cardiology (specializing in the heart)**
- **paediatrics (specializing in children's medicine)**
- **accident and emergency**
- **dermatology (specializing in the skin)**
- **ophthalmology (specializing in the eye)**
- **neurology (specializing in the brain).**

Nursing

Nurses work alongside doctors in hospitals, clinics, GP surgeries and can also work in health centres, schools, and private clinics, or they may travel around visiting patients in their homes. Nursing involves observing and monitoring patients, and planning and delivering treatment and care. As a nurse you may be needed to reassure frightened patients and their families, assist during operations, clean and dress wounds, give injections and other medication, and record information about patients.

MALE NURSES

In the past, nursing was thought to be a career for women. Today, only about 10 per cent of nurses are male, but this figure is increasing as more men are training to be nurses than ever before.

Nurses can specialize in many different areas of medicine.

- ◎ Elderly care nurses specialize in caring for the elderly.
- ◎ Mental health nurses help mentally ill patients.
- ◎ **Intensive care** nurses care for critically ill patients while they are in intensive care.
- ◎ Pain relief nurses provide pain relief during surgical operations and in hospital wards and give advice to people on how best to control pain.

below: *Dentists and dental nurses work closely together to care for their patients.*

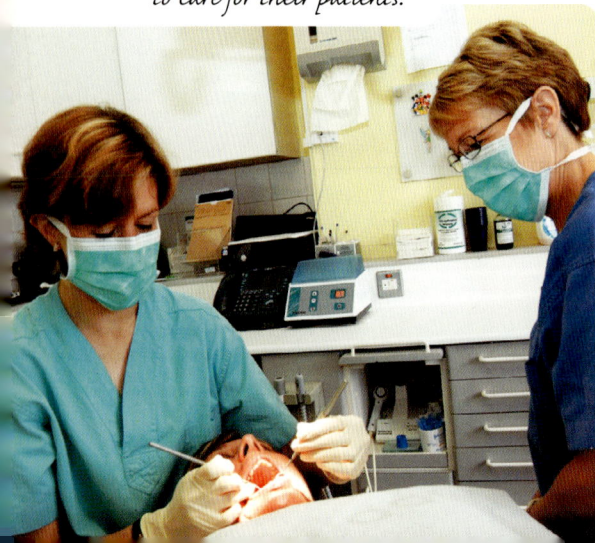

Midwifery

Midwives provide care and advice to pregnant women and their families. They help before, during, and after the pregnancy. All nurses and midwives are registered with the Nursing and Midwifery Council (NMC).

Dentistry

A dentist's main aim is to prevent tooth decay, but when problems arise dentists can treat them by inserting fillings, removing teeth, or fitting braces.

As well as dentists, you will find dental nurses, technicians, and hygienists also working in a dental surgery. Dental nurses assist the dentist and dental technicians make dental appliances such as dentures and braces. Dental hygienists remove plaque build-up from teeth and teach people how to care for their teeth and gums properly.

Dentists, dental nurses, and dental hygienists mainly work in private or NHS practices or in hospitals.

Healthcare science

Healthcare science includes a wide variety of jobs, some of which are described below.

Medical research scientists investigate the causes of diseases and undertake research to find new or better treatments. For example:

◎ **immunologists** examine the **immune system** and test **vaccines** such as those you may have had when you were a baby (tetanus, polio, measles, and mumps)
◎ microbiologists study **micro-organisms** that cause diseases and try to find cures
◎ virologists study all kinds of **viruses**, from the HIV virus to viruses responsible for the common cold.

Pharmacology is the study of drugs. Pharmacologists study how drugs work in the human body and what this reveals about how the body itself works. Clinical scientists test the effectiveness of new drugs in clinical trials on patients. **Pharmacists** work in chemists and make sure that drugs are supplied in the correct **dosage** to members of the public.

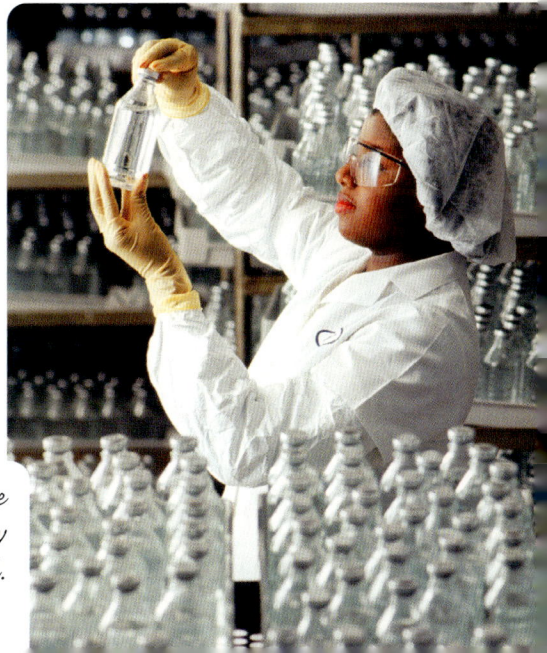

right: *Medical drugs are made in huge factories. The ingredients must be very carefully monitored and tested.*

Healthcare scientists work for hospitals, laboratories, drug companies, chemists, the Medical Research Council (MRC), and the government. Over the years, they have been responsible for the discovery of hundreds of drugs used in the treatment of diseases and the relief of human suffering.

HEALTHCARE TEAMWORK

Healthcare is about teamwork and many different people, from many different medical professions, may be involved in caring for a patient. If you broke your ankle in a rugby match, for example, you would first be attended to by a paramedic, who would arrive in an ambulance. Once at the hospital you would be cared for by doctors and nurses, and you would be transported around the hospital by hospital porters. You would also be seen by a **radiographer** who would take X-rays of the broken bone. You may require surgery in order to repair the break, and if so you would meet an **anaesthetist** who would put you to sleep before the operation, when the surgeon operates on you. You may then require the services of a **physiotherapist** in order to get your ankle moving properly again.

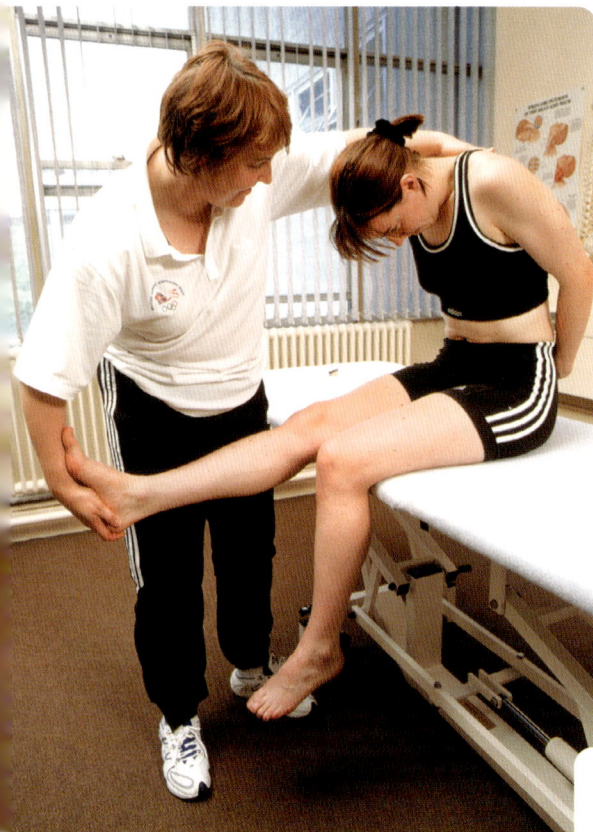

Some illnesses have long-term effects and therapists may be needed to help patients and their families cope. Therapists help people to cope with injuries, disabilities, or emotional problems. Physiotherapists are just one type of therapist, but there many other types, including speech therapists, who may help a **stroke** victim to regain his or her speech, and occupational therapists, who help people who cannot do everyday tasks due to illness or disability.

left: *Physiotherapists help patients along the road to full recovery.*

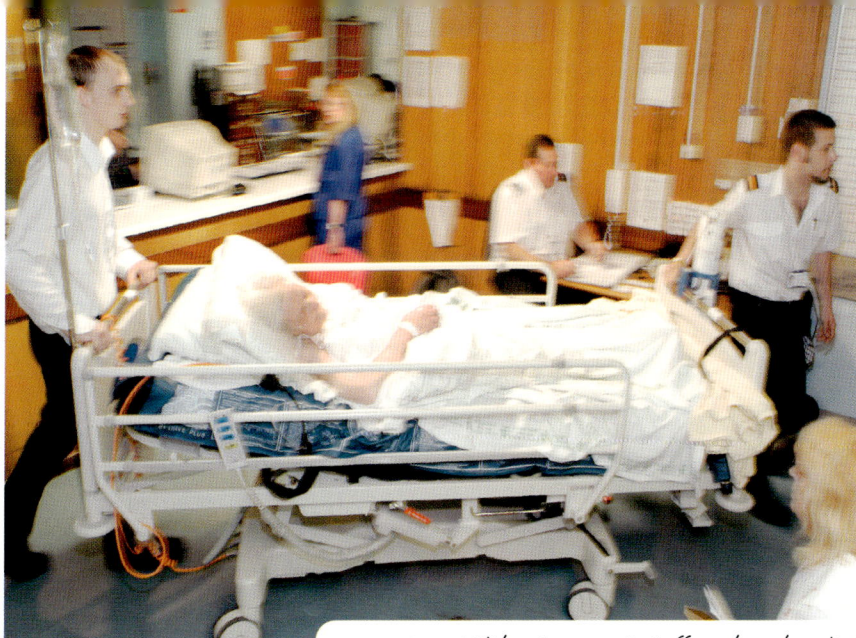

above: *Without support staff, such as hospital porters, hospitals and clinics would grind to a halt.*

Healthcare support staff

Hospitals and clinics do not only employ doctors and nurses. Behind the scenes there are a whole range of support jobs you can do. Hospitals and laboratories employ many different types of technical staff to provide modern technical procedures. Hospitals need porters to distribute essential supplies and to move patients around the hospital. They need administrators to maintain and update patient records. They also need catering and cleaning staff to provide meals and to keep the hospital clean.

Health education and promotion

Health education and health promotion workers aim to promote public health. Some may advise people on how to eat healthily or how to make lifestyle changes such as taking more exercise or giving up smoking. Others will educate the public in the signs and symptoms of various illnesses so that treatment can be given in time. A health education or promotion worker will give presentations to groups of people who may be at risk from illness or poor health. Health education or promotion specialists work for the NHS, health promotion agencies, charities, and local authorities.

Chapter 2

What types of jobs are available in the healthcare industry?

The healthcare industry offers a huge range of jobs, from anaesthetists to nurses to paramedics to therapists. Most jobs are concerned with caring for the sick or injured. Some involve working in a hospital or clinic dealing with patients on a day-to-day basis, whereas others are based in laboratories. Opportunities for work exist throughout the UK and there are jobs at all levels: management, professional, skilled, and semi-skilled.

Read through the following jobs and try to decide if any of them appeal to you. If they don't, this does not mean a career in the healthcare industry is not for you. This is just a small selection of the vast array of possible jobs that exist within the industry.

Doctors, nursing, and midwifery

General practitioner (GP)

You are likely to have made several visits to your general practitioner (GP), better known as your family doctor. GPs diagnose people's health problems in local communities. They will see and treat a huge variety of illnesses each week, some more serious that others. As a GP you will need to talk to and examine your patients to find out what is wrong with them. You would then prescribe medicine if necessary and give them advice on how to prevent getting ill in future. With more serious problems, you may need to refer the patients to a specialist at a hospital for further tests and treatment.

Mental health nurse

Mental health nurses play a vital part in helping GPs to care for people with mental health problems. They offer support, guidance, and advice to help people recognize the causes of their problems and identify coping strategies so they can lead as normal a life as possible.

Midwife

Midwives support women giving birth and can work in hospitals, clinics, and people's homes. Before the birth they will check the baby's development and mother's health, and offer counselling and help to the mother if required. They will also give advice to prospective parents on smoking, alcohol, and diet and how these can affect the health of the baby. As a midwife you will be present during the birth and help deliver the baby. You will offer help and advice to parents after the birth, and help new mothers suffering from **post-natal depression**.

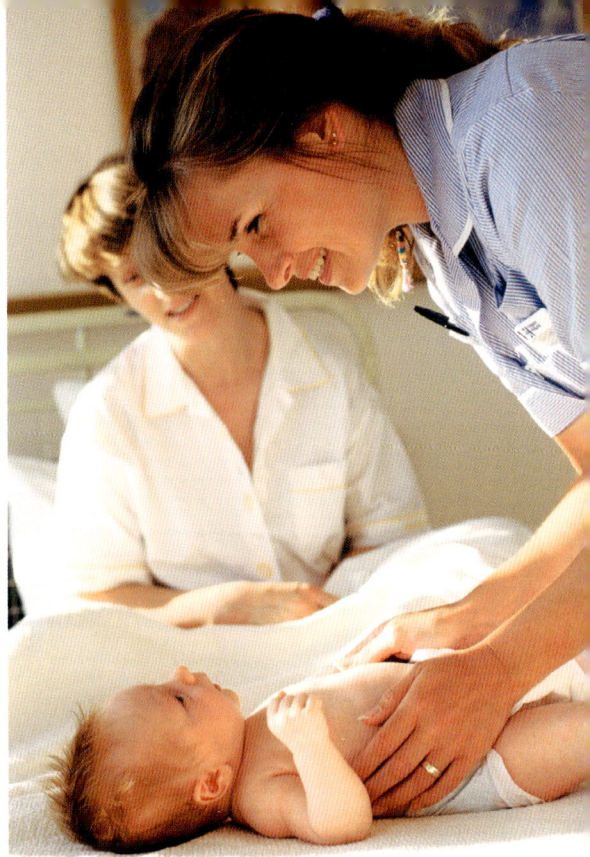

above: *Midwives are specially trained to look after new babies and mothers.*

Dentistry

General dental practitioner

A general dental practitioner (GDP) is the type of dentist you are likely to have visited as your family dentist. A GDP will examine your teeth and gums to find out if there are any problems. They will then decide if any treatment is necessary and, if so, provide the treatment. Their work may include removing teeth, inserting braces, and replacing fillings. A GDP will also be involved in running the dental practice.

Dental nurse

A dental nurse will assist a dentist. They may remove water and saliva from a patient's mouth while the dentist operates. They will **sterilize** and change the instruments and prepare materials for fillings. They may also record information about the patient and work on the reception desk.

Healthcare science

Pharmacist

You are most likely to have come into contact with the pharmacist who works in your local chemist. This is the person who will be given your prescription. They will provide you with the medicines you need, and give you advice on how to take them and the possible side effects. Pharmacists also work in hospitals and laboratories.

Pharmacologist

Pharmacologists work in laboratories and study the effects of drugs on people. As a pharmacologist you will carry out experiments, sometimes on animals or people, to measure the effectiveness of new drugs. You may also be involved in researching and discovering new drugs.

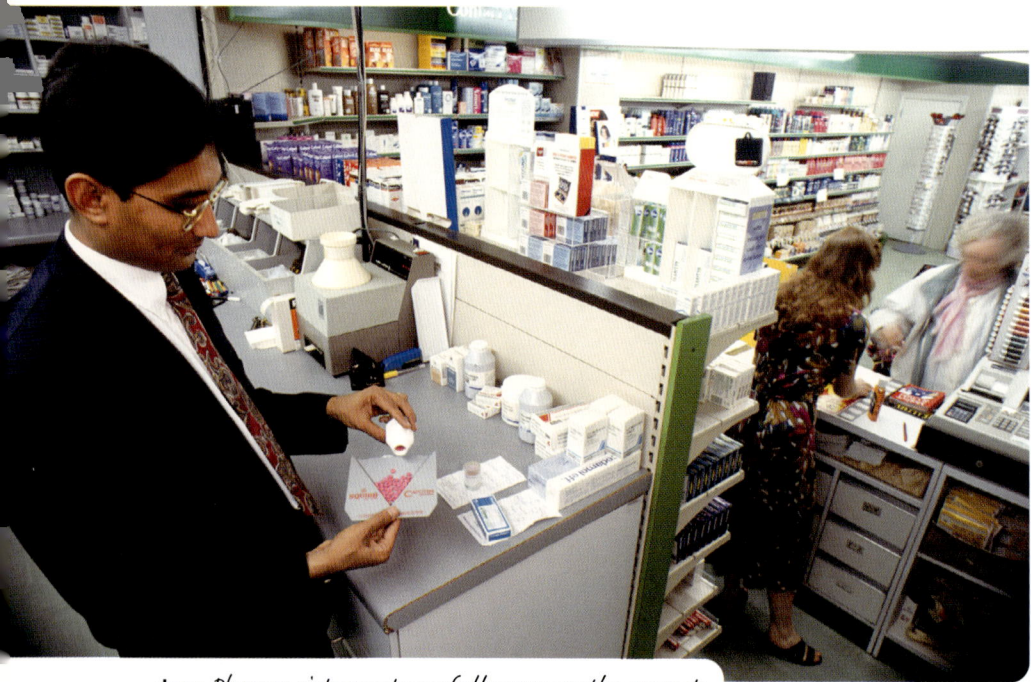

above: *Pharmacists must carefully prepare the correct prescription that the patient needs.*

Medical laboratory assistant

Medical laboratory assistants work in hospitals or research laboratories, helping scientists analyse medical samples or conduct research. As a laboratory assistant your job may include labelling samples, sterilising equipment, making up chemical solutions, and recording research results.

Other health professionals

Anaesthetist

An anaesthetist uses anaesthetic drugs to keep people asleep during surgery. Before surgery an anaesthetist will prepare the drugs and give the anaesthetic to the patient, according to the dosage required. As an anaesthetist you will need to reassure the patient while waiting for surgery. You will also care for the patient after surgery, and give them more pain relief if needed. Anaesthetists also give some types of pain relief to mothers during childbirth and patients in intensive care. All anaesthetists are qualified doctors who have done further training in anaesthetics.

above: *An anaesthetist gives a patient pain relief through an injection in the patient's back.*

Psychiatrist

All psychiatrists are qualified doctors who have done further training in psychiatry. They help people with mental health problems. Such problems can range from **depression** to eating disorders to drug abuse to **schizophrenia**. Some people with mental health problems, such as depression, can be looked after by their GP, but others need to be referred to a psychiatrist for further treatment.

As a psychiatrist you will talk to your patients and carry out tests to try to determine the cause of their problems. You will help the patients come to terms with their problems and understand them, decide on the best form of treatment and prescribe drugs if necessary.

Radiographer

Radiographers use X-ray machines to look inside the human body. They produce and **interpret** X-ray images of broken bones and other parts of the body. They will pass the images on to a doctor, who will then decide what treatment is necessary.

Paramedic

Paramedics are the people who arrive at accident sites, usually in ambulances. They are often the first people to treat patients who have been injured in an accident or who have suddenly fallen ill. Their job is to provide initial treatment to the casualties before taking them to hospital for further care. Paramedics are trained in emergency treatment and need to deal with casualties without delay to ensure they have the maximum chance of survival.

Physiotherapist

Physiotherapists treat physical problems caused by injuries to muscles, nerves, and bones. They will help people regain as much physical fitness and mobility as possible after illness or an accident. Most big sports teams, such as football and rugby clubs, employ a physiotherapist to help injured players get back to full fitness as soon as possible.

Physiotherapists also work in hospitals and health clinics, where they treat all sorts of problems caused by accidents, illness, or ageing. They help people to become mobile again after accidents such as a broken leg or wrist. They also work with stroke victims and people suffering from conditions such as **motor neurone disease**, to try to keep them as mobile as possible.

Healthcare support staff

Hospital porter

A hospital porter works in a hospital, transporting patients and equipment to where they are needed. You may need to wheel a patient in a bed from the ward to the anaesthetist's room, for example, before an operation. You may need to collect supplies of drugs from a delivery van and take them to the **pharmacy** in the hospital. Most employment available is in NHS hospitals, but there may also be some opportunities in private hospitals.

Get ahead!

Find out about three more jobs in the healthcare industry and list the main duties for each.

above: *Health promotion can prevent a lot of people from getting ill in the first place.*

Health education and promotion

Health promotion worker

A health promotion worker educates the public about any aspect to do with health. There are lots of different areas of health you could work in. You may work for a charity, for example, and your job may be to educate people about the signs and symptoms of **meningitis**. You may work with smokers and help them to give up smoking completely. Part of your job may involve you working in a school or office, promoting general health matters, such as diet and exercise, to the pupils or employees. Health visitors are qualified nurses who also specialize in the promotion of health and prevention of illness.

Get ahead!

Visit www.totaljobs.com and search for jobs under the heading "Health, nursing". Are there any jobs you would like to do?

Chapter 3

What will the working environment be like?

Do you like meeting new people every day or do you prefer to work alone? Do you like to know what you have to do each day or do you like surprises? In this section you will begin to get an idea of the working environment you can expect for jobs in healthcare.

Most people who want to work in healthcare do so because "they want to help people". However, there is much more to a job in the healthcare industry than this.

WHAT DO YOU WANT FROM YOUR CAREER?

You need to think about you career choice carefully. Different people want different things from their careers. You may want:

- a challenge
- a lot of money
- the security of having a job
- a chance to develop your skills
- the opportunity to meet lots of new people
- a chance to be part of a team
- the opportunity to travel.

Working conditions

Hospital staff

Hospital staff work as part of a team of doctors, nurses, specialists such as psychiatrists and anaesthetists, and support workers. Working hours for hospital doctors and nurses can be long and unsociable. You will usually work shifts and will often have to work night shifts and at weekends. As well as the long hours, these jobs can be physically demanding as you will be on your feet for most of the day and may be lifting or leaning over patients.

CASE STUDY

Anthony is a specialist doctor called a **dermatologist**. He works in a hospital.

I spend most of my time in an outpatient department. This consists of lots of consulting rooms where doctors see patients to discuss their skin problems.

About 1 or 2 days a week I do surgery to remove lumps from patients' skin. These lumps can range from skin cancers to moles. After I remove them they are sent to the laboratory to be examined under the microscope, to determine what they are.

Another part of my job involves going to see the in-patients (the patients who are in a ward in the hospital). These patients tend to be more sick and have more serious problems than the out-patients, so this aspect of the job is more challenging. I will review the patient and offer advice on managing the skin problem.

*The hours in dermatology are lighter than in many other medical specialties. The working day is pretty much 9.00 a.m. to 5.00 p.m., Monday to Friday. About once a week, I am **on call**. This means that I carry a pager with me for 24 hours and answer enquiries by telephone from other doctors about the skin problems their patients have.*

below: *Dermatologists deal with all sorts of skin problems.*

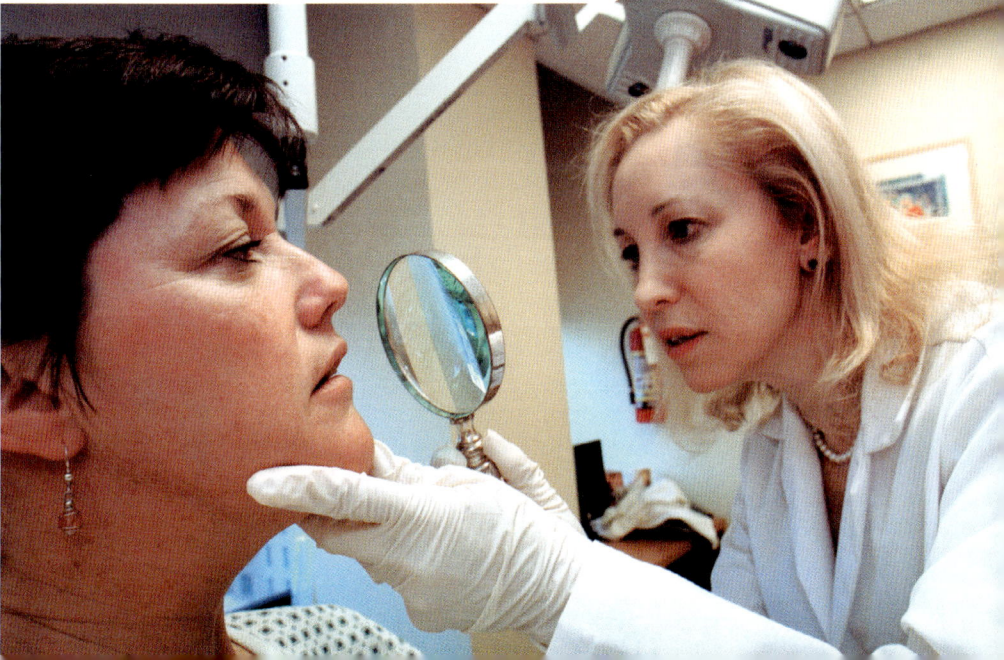

Hospital work can also be emotionally demanding as you may be working face to face with people who are seriously ill. You will also be dealing with their families, who may be upset and need constant support and comfort. Nurses may sometimes have challenging, practical, and "hands-on" tasks to do such as cleaning infected wounds and changing dirty bandages and dressings. Anaesthetists and radiologists will work with potentially dangerous chemicals and equipment.

GPs

Unlike hospital doctors, general practitioners (GPs) work in a surgery for most of the day, waiting for the patients to come to them. GPs usually work normal office hours, from Monday to Friday, and may have to work some Saturdays. As a GP you will also be on call some evenings and weekends. You will have to respond to emergency calls by visiting patients in their own homes. This could happen at any time of the night, and you have to be prepared to respond quickly whenever the phone rings.

below: *Staff at a GP surgery will deal with a wide range of patients.*

Dental staff

Most dentists are self-employed, and so can choose the hours they work. In general, a dentist and the other dental staff will work 9.00 a.m. to 5.00 p.m., Monday to Friday. A dentist may also have to work some evenings and weekends in order to carry out emergency treatment. Dentists may practise under the National Health Service or privately, but most dentists see a mixture of NHS and private patients.

As a dentist you will have to work very closely with your patients, often under bright lighting, and use specialist equipment that requires a steady hand. The work is demanding and there are risks involved in running your own business. However, the rewards can be good, both personally and financially.

WORKING ABROAD

Doctors, nurses, and dentists have good opportunities to work overseas, particularly in countries such as Australia and the United States. Doctors also have opportunities to work in less developed countries, where there may be limited healthcare facilities.

Physiotherapists

Physiotherapists work in a range of locations, such as hospitals, clinics, GP surgeries, and people's homes. As a physiotherapist your job will be physically demanding as you may need to assist patients with mobility or help them to move their joints. It can also be emotionally demanding, because you may have to encourage patients to do exercises they find very painful. You will mainly work normal office hours, but may need to work some evenings and weekends.

Paramedics

Paramedics and other ambulance workers will be based in an ambulance station, but will spend most of their time travelling between accident sites and hospitals. They work shifts, so as a paramedic you will be expected to work some nights and weekends. You will also work outdoors a lot of the time, in all weather conditions, and you may have to cope with upsetting situations.

right: *Being a paramedic can be physically and emotionally demanding, especially when dealing with large accidents.*

Healthcare scientists

Healthcare scientists work in laboratories and work 9.00 a.m. to 5.00 p.m. For most laboratory work you are likely to need to wear protective clothing, such as a lab coat and gloves, especially when handling chemicals. Some research posts involve you sitting at a computer for most of the day.

Health promotion

Heath promotion workers work normal office hours but have to be prepared to work some weekends, for example, to help out at charity or educational events. You will be based in an office, but there is likely to be a lot of travelling involved in your job, as you have to make presentations to various groups, such as schools and community groups in different areas.

A typical working day?

Some jobs will not have a typical working day. Most hospital jobs involve working long, unsociable hours, including nights and weekends. Doctors, nurses and specialists will have to deal with new patients every day and no two days will be the same. On the other hand, for those working in laboratories or offices, a normal 9.00 a.m. to 5.00 p.m. weekly routine is more likely.

below: *Patients still need care and attention during the night!*

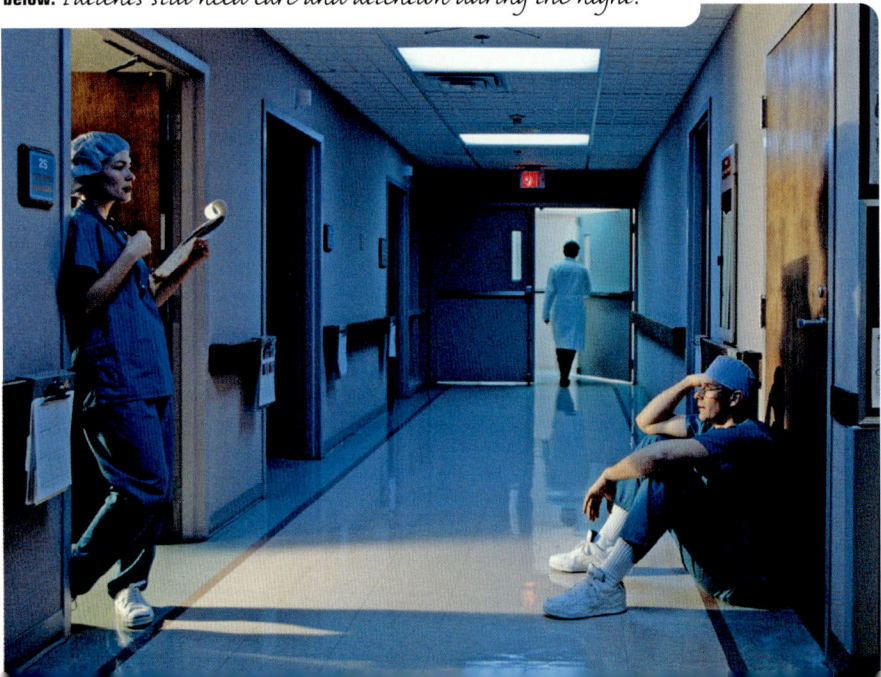

The best people to tell you about a typical working day in the healthcare industry are those who work in it. Below are some examples.

Emma is an information and education officer for a meningitis charity.

*A typical day consists of taking calls from people concerned about meningitis, reassuring them, and sending out the relevant information. If there has been a case of meningitis I will contact the school or workplace and offer advice and support. Sometimes people need more help, especially if they have lost someone close, so I direct them to **bereavement** counselling. I find this the most distressing part of the job. I also give awareness talks on meningitis to groups such as nursing students, mother and toddler groups, nursery school staff, and university students. I often have to travel to give these talks, but one of the perks of the job is that my employer's give me a car.*

Aida is a dental nurse at a private dental surgery.

I check the list of appointments for the day on the computer as soon as I arrive at work. I also check that all items needed for the day's patients are back from the lab; this could include dentures or braces. I then set out the sterile equipment ready for the first patient. Most of my day is spent either assisting the dentist with patients or dealing with enquiries on the reception desk. The work is quite varied, so no two days are ever the same.

Imran is a radiographer in a hospital.

I work shifts and do not really have a typical day. I also have to be on call some weekends to deal with any emergencies that come in. I spend most of my time meeting patients and taking X-rays. As radiation is dangerous I have to wear a protective apron. I then have to interpret the X-rays, along with a specialist doctor called a radiologist. I will write up the records for each patient.

How much will I get paid?

For some people, this is the most important question when deciding on a career. Rates of pay vary a lot depending on your specific job, where you work, your experience, and your qualifications.

Doctors and specialists

Financial rewards for doctors and specialists are good. Newly qualified doctors working in a hospital can expect to earn upwards from £30,000 per year. Newly qualified specialists, such as psychiatrists and anaesthetists, can expect to start on slightly more than this. The average salary for a hospital doctor with a few years experience is £50,000 per year. GP salaries range from around £40,000 to £80,000 per year.

above: *For many people in the healthcare industry, the rewards are about much more than money.*

Nursing

Few people work in nursing for the money, although today, nurses can earn reasonable wages. A newly qualified nurse or midwife will earn £17,000 per year, rising to £25,000 with experience. Specialist nurses and nurse managers can earn much more.

Dentistry

Dentists, when fully trained, can earn £50,000 to £70,000 per year, although they will start on around £26,000 per year. Dental nurses will earn around £12,000 to £17,000, but wages in private practices vary greatly.

Healthcare science

Once qualified, pharmacists and pharmacologists can earn £20,000 to £50,000, depending on experience. As a medical laboratory assistant you can expect to start on £10,000 to £13,000.

Chapter 4

Am I the right person for the job?

Before you go any further, take the time to answer the following questions:

◎ Do you enjoy helping people with their problems and their pain?
◎ Do you enjoy learning and gaining new understanding?
◎ Are you interested in how the human body functions?
◎ Are you interested in how medicine can be used to improve life?

If you answered "yes" to any of these questions, the chances are you have the right kind of personality for a career in healthcare.

People skills

The ability to get on well with people is important in most jobs, and the healthcare industry is no exception. In a hospital you will need to be able to work closely with others, both patients and other members of staff. You will probably be working as part of a team with other healthcare professionals and technicians, so will need to have good teamwork skills.

Get ahead!

As you read the information in this chapter, think carefully about your own personality and your likes and dislikes.

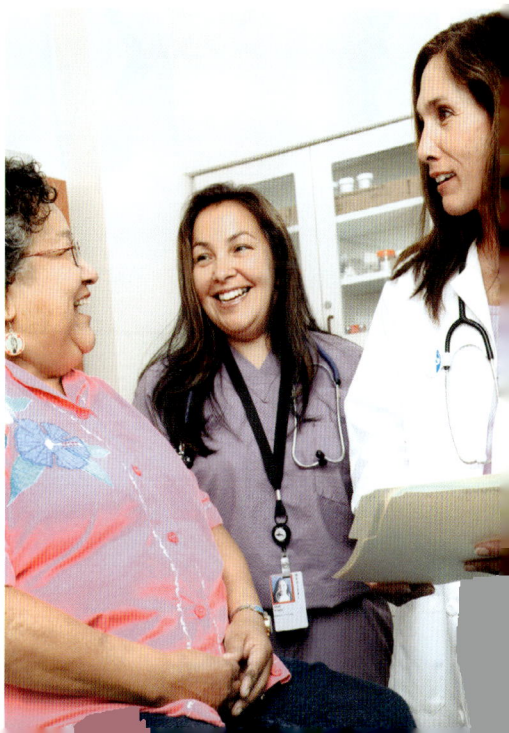

right: *Healthcare workers need to like people and have an interest in their welfare.*

CASE STUDY

Saskia is a hospital doctor.

The ability to work within a team is absolutely crucial to my job. When I do my rounds I check the patients with other doctors and members of the nursing staff. To succeed as a doctor you have to want to do it. It is difficult if a patient doesn't make it, as you can't help feeling responsible. Some people can't deal with this kind of pressure. You need to be kind, patient, and have good listening skills. Being a doctor is hard work. I am on my feet most of the day and I have to stay focused. It can be very draining.

Communication skills

You need to have excellent communication skills for any job in the healthcare industry.

◎ As a doctor, psychiatrist, dentist, or pharmacist you will need to explain things to patients in terms they can understand.
◎ Nursing is as much about communication skills as applying bandages. The ability to listen and to explain a situation clearly and accurately to a doctor is a core nursing requirement.
◎ In health promotion work you need to be able to get your message across in clear, appropriate language so that everyone can understand.
◎ Healthcare scientists will need good communication skills for presenting their work and writing up their research.

left: *Healthcare support staff, such as hospital receptionists, need to be able to deal politely with people.*

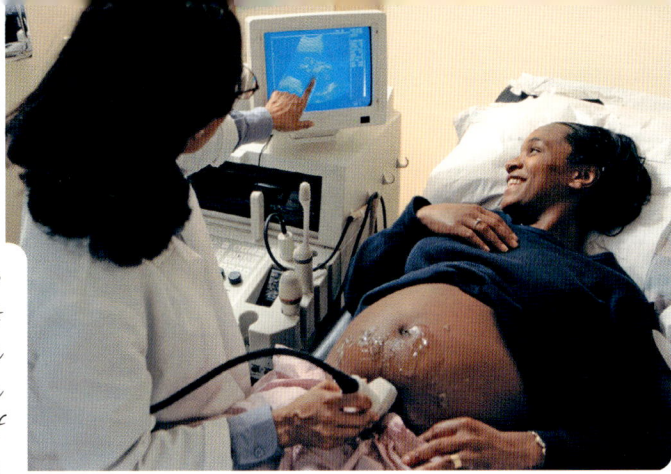

right: *You need to have excellent communication skills to explain all aspect's of patient care.*

Additional skills

You need to be flexible and adaptable, as your job will constantly be changing, and you may have to deal with new situations all the time. Sometimes these unforeseen situations may be emergencies. Doctors, specialists, and nurses must be able to respond quickly to any changes in a patient's condition. As well as having the scientific knowledge required to do the job, they must also be observant and pay attention to detail. They must be able to keep calm and work under pressure. All healthcare professionals need to be quick thinking and decisive, but also provide a reassuring environment for patients and relatives.

DEALING WITH THE PUBLIC

You should have a smart appearance for jobs that involve dealing with the public a lot of the time. You also need to be friendly and approachable, as you will be expected to help people, provide them with information, and answer their questions. Doctors and dentists are respected members of society and as such should act professionally at all times.

CASE STUDY

Jenny is a health promotion worker.

The ability to communicate with a wide range of groups, from healthcare professionals to small community groups, is very important in my job. Written as well as oral communication is vital to get your message across, for example, when writing press releases and talking to journalists. In my job listening skills are also important as I spend a lot of time with people who have been affected by poor health.

CONFIDENTIALITY

You need to be trustworthy for any job in the healthcare industry where you are dealing with patients. You will often be given confidential information about a patient; this cannot be discussed with anyone else other than the people you are working with.

Stamina

As working hours for hospital doctors and nurses can be long and unsociable, a huge amount of discipline, energy, and mental toughness are needed for the job. You need to be self-confident in your decisions at all times, even when you are tired.

Counselling skills

Counsellors and therapists must have personal qualities such as patience, **persistence**, and the ability to help people face difficult situations. This type of work involves considerable emotional strain, so clear thinking and sound judgement is needed, together with sensitivity, **tolerance**, and a responsible attitude.

Technical skills

Healthcare scientists and radiographers use technical equipment and computers in their work, so they must have good technical and IT skills. Pharmacists and other medical scientists also need an eye for detail, for preparing and measuring medicines or for conducting research experiments. Dentists and surgeons need good eyesight and good manual skills, in other words, a steady hand!

CASE STUDY

Ahmed is a paramedic.

Ambulance staff deal with people who may be very distressed, so a responsible, caring, and calm attitude helps. Listening to patients is also very important. I work as part of a team and good communication skills are essential in order to deal with emergencies quickly and effectively. I often have to make serious decisions quickly, such as taking control of the situation at the scene of an accident, so leadership skills are important. You also need to be physically fit as there will be a lot of lifting, and you definitely cannot be squeamish.

Staying power

Finally, most healthcare professionals, including doctors and specialists such as anaesthetists and psychiatrists, must be prepared to undertake a long programme of education and training in order to gain the in-depth knowledge required to do their jobs.

right: *Many medical procedures require a steady hand and a high level of accuracy.*

CASE STUDY

Lidia is an anaesthetist working in a hospital.

Hard work and perseverance are essential in this line of work, and you must be prepared to make many personal sacrifices in your family and social life to succeed. Kindness should also not be underestimated as a quality in doctors. No matter how much you know, or how much expertise you have in a certain field, you will be dealing with people at their most vulnerable. You can make their experience of the healthcare industry more pleasant by being kind and sensitive in your dealings with them.

Finding the right job for you

Finding the best career for you involves matching your skills and personality to the skills needed for a particular job. The best way to do this is to start by taking a close look at yourself.

◎ Do you really care about people's health?
◎ Are your communication skills strong?
◎ Do you cope well under pressure?
◎ Do you enjoy working with people?

SKILLS CHECKLIST

Copy out and fill in the checklist of skills below. Look back at the information in this chapter to see if your skills match up with those required by jobs in the healthcare industry. Can you identify any area of the industry that you are particularly suited to?

Skills required	Yes (✔)	No (✔)	Especially important for:
Enjoy working with people	☐	☐	All healthcare jobs
Care for people's health	☐	☐	All healthcare jobs
Good communication skills	☐	☐	All healthcare jobs
Flexible and adaptable	☐	☐	Doctors, nurses, paramedics
Good laboratory skills	☐	☐	Healthcare scientists
Good research skills	☐	☐	Healthcare scientists
Responsible	☐	☐	All healthcare jobs
Able to remain calm under pressure	☐	☐	Doctors, nurses, paramedics
Able to deal with emergencies	☐	☐	Doctors, nurses, paramedics
Quick thinking and decisive	☐	☐	Doctors, nurses, paramedics
Work well in a team	☐	☐	All healthcare jobs
Able to cope with long hours	☐	☐	Doctors and nurses

Get ahead!

Draw a table with the following headings:
• work well under pressure
• attention to detail
• team working
• communication skills
Under each heading, write down the things you have done that show you have these skills.

So, do you think you are the right person for a career in healthcare? If you have a caring, responsible attitude, with good communication skills, you are on the right track!

Chapter 5

What qualifications do I need?

Now you know what kind of person would be best suited to working in the healthcare industry, but what qualifications do you need?

Some jobs in the healthcare industry, such as doctors and dentists, require a high level of qualifications just to get in. You will then need to undertake a long period of intensive study in order to qualify fully. By gaining a recognized qualification, either through training at work or by taking a full-time course at university, you are likely to have a much wider range of career opportunities and better chances of **promotion**.

There is a whole range of qualifications that can help prepare you for entry to healthcare jobs. These range from GCSEs, **National Vocational Qualifications** (NVQs) and **Scottish Vocational Qualifications** (SVQs), A-levels and Highers, to degrees and postgraduate qualifications. You need to think about what you want to do within the healthcare industry, then you can decide which qualifications are most suitable.

WHICH QUALIFICATION?

◎ NVQs/ SVQs in Healthcare: provide a flexible approach to studying a number of different subjects and allow you to progress at your own pace. They have been developed to prepare you for a variety of jobs in the healthcare industry. You can gain NVQs/ SVQs by taking a full-time course at college, or you can study part-time while at work.

◎ Modern **Apprenticeships** in Health and Administration: provide an opportunity to develop skills and expertise and gain NVQs/SVQs while at work.

◎ Further and Higher Education: Many universities and some colleges offer Higher National Certificate (HNC), Higher National Diploma (HND), or degree courses in Medicine, the sciences, and other related subject areas.

For the jobs given below, there is no single entry route. The qualifications described are the most common and most relevant for the particular job, but are by no means the only qualifications you could consider.

Doctor

Becoming a doctor is hard work. Entry into medical school is very competitive. There will be a lot of applications for a limited number of places each year, so you need to do well to get in. Most medical schools will want excellent GCSE and A-level/Higher results, and will accept no other form of qualification. You will need three A-levels or three Advanced Highers at grades ABB or higher, including two sciences, usually Chemistry and Biology, and one other subject.

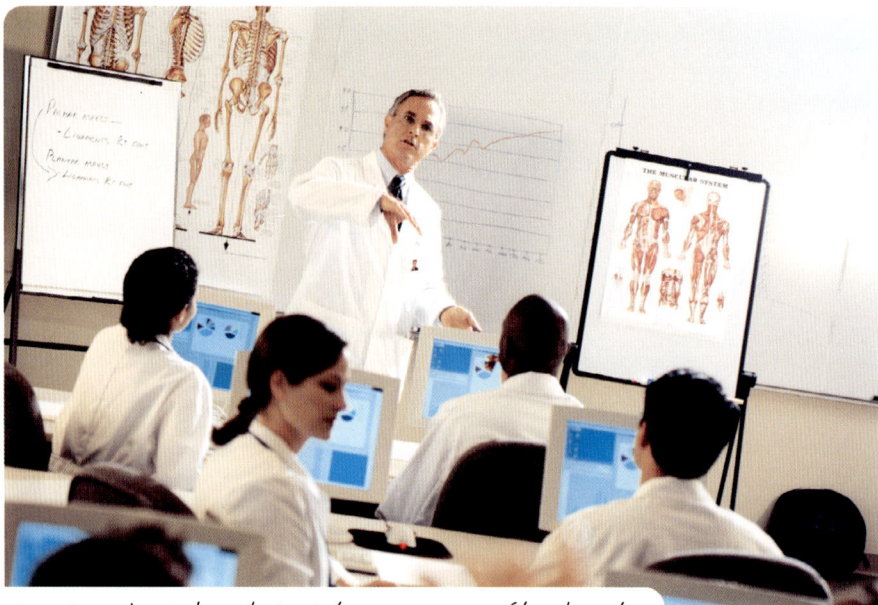

above: *Learning to be a doctor takes many years of hard work.*

Once you get into medical school, training is intensive and qualification takes five years. If you want to take responsibility for people's health and well-being you have to be serious about learning. During your medical degree you will spend a lot of time working in hospitals, gaining real-life experience. You must therefore be sure that this is what you want to do and realistic about your abilities before you apply.

After you graduate from medical school you will need to work in a hospital for 1 year. You will then be able to register with the General Medical Council (GMC), which means you are finally allowed to practise medicine. Once you are qualified you will then specialize in the area of medicine that most interests you.

If you decide to become a GP – and almost half of qualified doctors do – you will need to work in hospitals, in different areas of medicine, for 2 years. You will then need to work in a GP practice for a further year, supervised by a GP trainer, and take exams at the end of the year.

Psychiatry

To become a psychiatrist you first need to qualify and register as a doctor. If you decide to concentrate on psychiatric medicine you will then have to study and train for 3 more years.

CASE STUDY

Anastasia is a GP in a local health centre.

*After A-levels I did a 5-year medical degree. I then worked as a hospital doctor for 1 year in order to gain General Medical Council **accreditation**. After this I did some 6-month training blocks in paediatrics, geriatrics, and accident and emergency medicine. I then worked as a trainee GP in a surgery for 1 year before becoming a member of the Royal College of General Practitioners. I started my current job 5 years ago.*

CASE STUDY

Juan is a dermatologist in a hospital.

After A-levels I went to medical school where, after 6 years, I was awarded the degrees MB (Bachelor of Medicine), BCh (Bachelor of Surgery), BAO (Bachelor of Obstetrics), and BMedSci (Bachelor of Medical Science). This entitles you to begin working as a doctor. Over the course of the first 3 years of working as a doctor, I had to do three further exams in order to gain my MRCP (Membership of the Royal College of Physicians). This qualification entitles you to train in a medical speciality such as dermatology.

Anaesthetist

To become an anaesthetist you first need to qualify and register as a doctor. You will then need to spend 5 years working as a specialist in anaesthesia. Once you qualify you will be awarded the Certificate of Completion of Specialist Training (CCST) which enables you to work as a **consultant**.

Nursing and midwifery

To get into nursing college you will need five GCSEs (grades A–C) or S-grades (1–3), including English, Maths and Science. You will also need either two A-levels or Highers in science subjects, or vocational qualifications such as NVQs or SVQs.

To qualify as a nurse takes 4 years. In the last 2 years of study you will choose to specialize in an area such as mental health, adult, or child medicine. You will spend half of your time working in hospitals or in the community working in care homes, clinics, and people's homes. Once you have qualified you will be able to register with the Nursing and Midwifery Council (NMC). You can then specialize further, with more training. You could become an ophthalmic nurse, for example, providing nursing support for eye clinics.

below: *Nurses are required to learn a huge amount so they have the knowledge to back up their practical skills.*

Robert is a mental health nurse.

I did an NVQ in Health and Social Care and then voluntary work for a centre for children with special needs. I then managed to get on to a nursing degree course and did a BSc in Mental Health Nursing. Because I don't have A-levels, I don't think I would have been accepted unless I had the work experience behind me.

Dentistry

Dentists

Like a medical degree, a degree in dentistry also takes 5 years, so you need to be absolutely certain this is what you want to do before setting out on this career path. Also like medicine, competition for places is strong, so academic requirements are high. You will need three science A-levels or three Advanced Highers at grades ABB or higher. The degree course includes academic education combined with practical training in all aspects of dental practice. On qualifying and before being able to practise, dentists must register with the General Dental Council.

Dental nurses and technicians

There are no set entry requirements for dental nurses and dental technicians, but a good general education is normally required – four GCSEs grades (A–C) or S-grades (1–3), including English and Biology. You will usually study towards qualifications part-time while working. Nurses can study for the National Certificate of Dental Nursing, and technicians can study for a Higher National Diploma (HND) in dental technology.

Alex works as a self-employed dental hygienist.

I left school at 16 and took a nursing course as I'd always wanted to be a midwife. I then changed my mind and enrolled on a 2-year full-time dental hygienist course. I worked for different dental practices for 5 years before becoming self-employed. I now work for three different practices.

Medical research scientists

Most medical research jobs require a university degree in a related field. University entry requirements vary, but you will usually need at least GCSE/S-grade Maths and A-levels/Highers in Biology and Chemistry.

There are no formal entry requirements to work as a medical lab assistant but four GCSEs (grades A–C) or S-grades (grades 1–3) may be an advantage. Most training is done on the job and lab assistants can work towards an NVQ/SVQ in Clinical Laboratory Support.

To study pharmacology, a degree is essential. In order to get on to a degree course you will need A-levels or Highers in Chemistry, Biology and Physics, or Maths. **Sandwich courses** are available at some universities, which include 1 year working in industry. These enable students to get direct experience of working. Many pharmacology graduates go on to undertake further qualifications, such as MScs and PhDs, which are usually necessary for research careers.

The only route into pharmacy is through gaining a Master of Pharmacy degree. Entry requirements are five GCSEs (grades A–C) or S-grades (grades 1–3), including English and Maths, as wells as three good science A-levels or Highers.

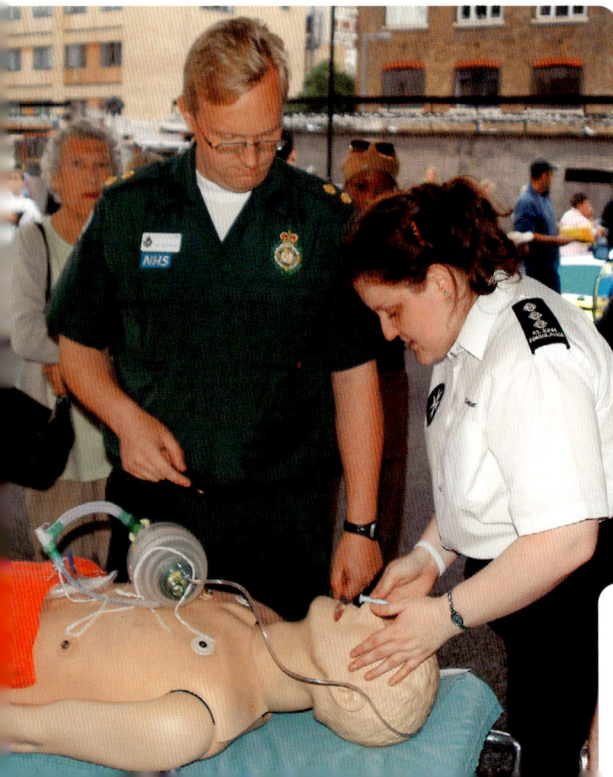

Paramedic

To become a paramedic you would normally be expected to work as an ambulance care assistant first. For this you will need a clean driving licence and you will have to pass an entrance exam. At least four GCSEs (grades A–C) or S-grades (grades 1–3), including English and Maths, may also be required.

left: *Paramedics must continue to learn about new techniques and procedures once they are qualified.*

Once you are 21 you can progress to become an ambulance technician, and after a year's experience you can become a paramedic. In order to become a paramedic you will also need to pass the Institute of Health Care and Development (IHCD) exams and be registered with the Health Professionals Council.

Radiography

Entry requirements for a radiography degree are usually five GCSEs (grades A–C) or S-grades (grades 1–3) including English and Maths, and two A-levels or Highers in science subjects. Once qualified, radiographers must register with the Health Professionals Council.

Physiotherapy

To become a physiotherapist you will need a degree in Physiotherapy and membership of the Chartered Society of Physiotherapy. Competition for degree places is usually fierce so you will need three good A-level or Highers grades (most institutions require at least one science A-level or Higher), or equivalent NVQs.

Healthcare support staff

Some technical roles require professional qualifications or specialist skills. For other jobs, such as porters and administration staff, good communication skills, teamwork, and a willingness to learn are more important than formal qualifications. For the job of hospital porter, you may need a driving licence and you will often be required to pass a medical exam or fitness test.

Get ahead!

Find a copy of a local newspaper. Identify as many jobs in healthcare as you can. For each job, list the skills and qualifications you would need.

YOUR PERSONALITY ALSO MATTERS!

Qualifications alone are no guarantee of a job in the healthcare industry – much depends on your personality, attitude, communication skills, and common-sense approach to work and life in general.

Chapter 6

A foot in the door

You have a good understanding of science, enjoy working with people, and have excellent communication skills. You seem like the ideal candidate for a position in the healthcare industry . . . but how do you set about actually getting a job?

Do well at school

Whatever job you are applying for in the healthcare industry, most employers look for a good standard of secondary education, including GCSEs (grades A–C) or S-grades (1–3) in English, Maths, and science subjects.

Your mathematical and English skills will be important in any job that you do. As a doctor, nurse, or dentist you will need to be good with numbers, so that you can give the correct doses of medication to patients. In a medical laboratory you may need excellent mathematical skills to use complex equations and computer modelling software. You mathematical skills will also be important for most jobs for dealing with **statistics**, e.g. patient numbers.

below: *Pay attention in your chemistry lessons if you want to work in healthcare!*

Good English skills will be needed for writing formal letters, reports, and sending information round to work colleagues. If you have to speak to groups as part of your job, your oral presentation skills also need to be good. Other subjects, such as History and Business Studies, will also give you useful communication skills. Psychology will be useful for work involving counselling, therapy, and health promotion.

For a career in healthcare you will need to have a good understanding of science. An ability in Chemistry and Biology (and to a lesser extent Physics) is therefore important. Biology and Chemistry are particularly important for knowing how the human body works.

COMMUNICATION SKILLS

For any job in the healthcare industry it would be beneficial to work in any environment where you are involved in meeting a lot of different people, for example, working in a shop or as a receptionist. This way, you can develop your communication skills.

The importance of work experience

A relevant qualification will be vital to your employment prospects. However, another key factor that employers will be looking for is relevant experience, especially experience of working with people, so you should try to gain some before applying for jobs. There are plenty of things you can do while you are still at school or college that could improve your chances of getting into your chosen career.

◎ If you see yourself as a nurse, try to get some experience of working with people in a caring role. You could volunteer to help out at your local youth club, offer to baby-sit, or care for an elderly relative. You could also apply for more specialist work experience in a hospital or nursing home.

◎ To show your commitment to becoming a doctor or a dentist, try to spend some time in your local doctor or dentist surgery, either **work shadowing** the GP or dentist, or helping out on the reception desk.

◎ If you would like to get into health promotion, try to gain some relevant experience working for a health company. This will provide you with good practice of talking to people about sensitive health issues.

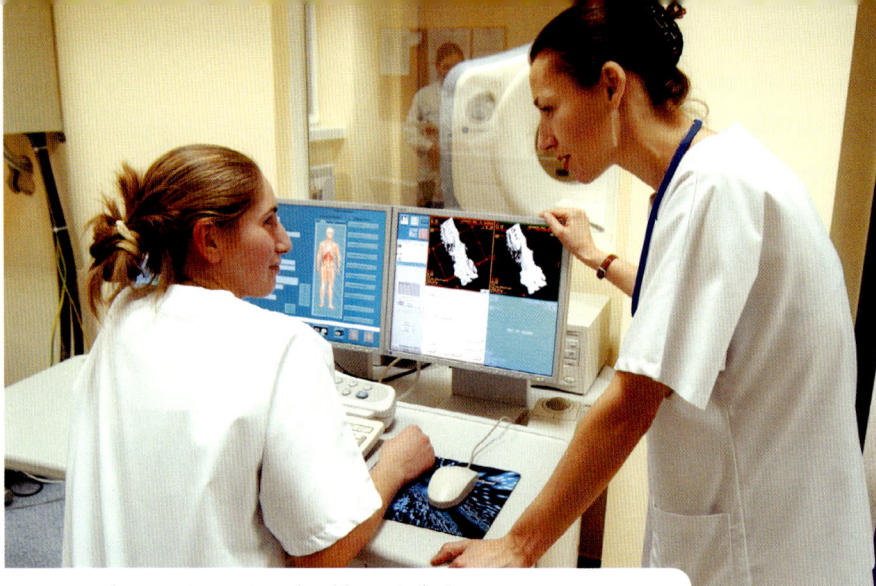

above: *Work experience is valuable as it helps you to work out if you would like a career in healthcare.*

The job for you?

Any work experience, whether it is a placement organized by your school or part-time work you have organized yourself, will give you an idea of what the job itself is like and the reality of a working life. This gives you the chance to find out whether this is actually what you want to do as a career.

How to stand out from the crowd

BENEFITS OF WORK EXPERIENCE

Work experience will show employers that you are keen and have made an effort to find out about work before applying for a job. It will also make you appear more confident, due to the extra knowledge and skills you will have gained.

Getting a job in the healthcare industry will be very difficult. There may be lots of enthusiastic, highly qualified young people competing for a limited number of jobs. It is therefore not enough to have the relevant qualifications and work experience – you need to stand out from the crowd.

Employers usually look for a broad range of personal skills, including teamwork skills, being self-motivated, and having good communication skills, so think about what you have to offer.

Applying for jobs

To find out what jobs are on offer in the healthcare industry, you can search in a number of places.

- Look in newspapers, both local and national, for job adverts.
- Talk to your careers advisor at school.
- Visit the careers section of your local library.
- Look for the names of companies that you might be interested in working for on the Internet and in brochures. You can then write to them to see if they have any suitable work.
- Search the Internet for jobs. See page 51 for some useful websites.
- Visit job centres and recruitment agencies.

Some examples of the types of job vacancies you might see in your local paper are shown below.

Radiographer

Salary: Depends on experience

We are a well established company, providing comprehensive mobile imaging services. We provide a busy, challenging, and satisfying working environment, with state of the art equipment.

You will be working in a busy mobile radiography unit using technical equipment. You will be expected to write reports where appropriate and order relevant films and other materials where necessary. You must possess a suitable qualificati... in Radiography, a full driving licence, and have access to a car.

Healthcare Technical Officer

Salary: £11,879 – £14,739 pa

Working hours: Monday to Friday, 8.30a.m.–4.45p.m.

You will be expected to work on a wide range of tasks, supporting qualified scientists in their work. Your role will include processing blood donations, using specialized laboratory equipment, and keeping computerised records up to date.

The job demands excellent team working skills, meticulous attention to detail, and the ability to precisely follow written instructions. Ideally, we would also like to see GCSEs at grades C or above in Maths and English or another equivalent qualification such as an NVQ.

When you apply for a job, you will either have to fill in an application form or provide a curriculum vitae (CV). This will be the first impression the employer has of you, so you need to get it right.

Completing application forms

If the employer sends you an application form, then you must use this to apply for the job. The first thing you should do is photocopy the form, so you can create a rough draft on the photocopy. This way, if you make any mistakes, it does not matter.

Read through all the questions before you start, and then take your time to fill in the answers. Make sure you answer the questions actually asked and always be honest. If you make things up, the chances are you will be found out if you make it to the interview stage.

Before you fill in your application form, write down everything you think the employer will want to see evidence of. Then add the skills you have that are relevant to those required by the employer.

Once you have checked your draft form for spelling mistakes, grammar, and punctuation, you can copy it on to the original application form. Keep your writing neat and tidy and check the form again before sending it off – or better still, get someone else to check it for you. Make sure you post it well before the closing date and use a suitable envelope.

Follow all the instructions on the form.

Make sure you begin with your most recent job or placement.

Include any part-time work you have done.

State why you are interested in the job.

Describe any relevant hobbies you may have.

Include any relevant skills and experience that you have not already mentioned.

APPLICATION FORM
Please use black ink

Job title

PERSONAL DETAILS
First name   Surname
                          Date of birth
Address
                          Phone number
                          E-mail address
Post code

WORK EXPERIENCE
Include any work experience or voluntary work.

Employer's name	Your title	Dates of employment From To

QUALIFICATIONS

Subject/Course	Level (Standard, Higher, SVQ, Unit, Other)	Year taken	Final result

PERSONAL PROFILE
Use this space to give any additional information that may be of interest to the employer.

REFERENCE
Please provide the name and address of someone who can be asked for a reference.

Name and job title	Address	Telephone number

I confirm that the information on this form is true and correct to the best of my knowledge.

Signature   Date

CVs and covering letters

A CV tells employers about your education, experience, and interests. Some employers will ask for a CV instead of sending you an application form to fill in. When you write your CV you will need to include all the information that the employer would have requested from you on an application form. You will also need to send a covering letter explaining why you are applying for the job.

An example of a CV is shown below. As you can see, it has been typed and has a clear layout. Firstly, it gives your personal details, such as your name, address, and school. It then describes your qualifications, work experience, and interests.

Get ahead!

Copy out and fill in the application form on page 42, using as many of the following phrases as possible. They are all things employers will like to see on your application form.
- enthusiastic
- hard working
- good at writing and speaking clearly
- honest
- good at working in a team
- reliable
- willing to learn.

Oliver Malcolm

Date of birth	10 October 1988
Address	40 Spalding Road Birmingham B22 9FG
Telephone	0121 610 4912
Email	omalcolm@email.net
School	Damhead School Birmingham B18 7JN 1998–2006

Make sure all details are correct.

EDUCATION

Subject	Qualification	Result
Geography	A level	C
Business Studies	A level	C
Science	A level	C
Maths	GCSE	B
English	GCSE	B
History	GCSE	C
Science	GCSE	C
French	GCSE	A
Art	GCSE	C
Geography	GCSE	A

Put your most recent qualifications first.

Remember to include any work experience.

EMPLOYMENT/WORK EXPERIENCE

2006–2007 Elderly care nurse at Broomhill Park.
2006 Work experience (3 weeks) serving customers in a doctor's surgery.

INTERESTS

I am a member of the school gymnastics and swimming team.
I play the piano (Grade 6) and guitar (Grade 4).
I have the Pool Bronze award from the Royal Life Saving Society.

Try to include relevant interests and include any positions of responsibility, for example, team captain.

REFEREE

Mr J Downing
Form Teacher
Damhead School
Birmingham B18 7JN

A teacher is a good person to use as a **referee** – make sure you ask their permission first.

Get ahead!

Write down some examples of your skills that fall into the following categories:

- dealing with people
- team work
- practical skills
- organizing.

Now write your CV, trying to include evidence of as many of these skills as possible. They are all things that employers will want to see on your CV.

You should always send a handwritten or typed covering letter with your CV that explains why you are applying for the job. You need to make your covering letter specific to the job you are applying for. Always address it to a specific person – never write "Dear Sir/Madam" (you may need to contact the organization by telephone to find out who to address it to). In your letter you should show that you know something about the company. An example is shown below.

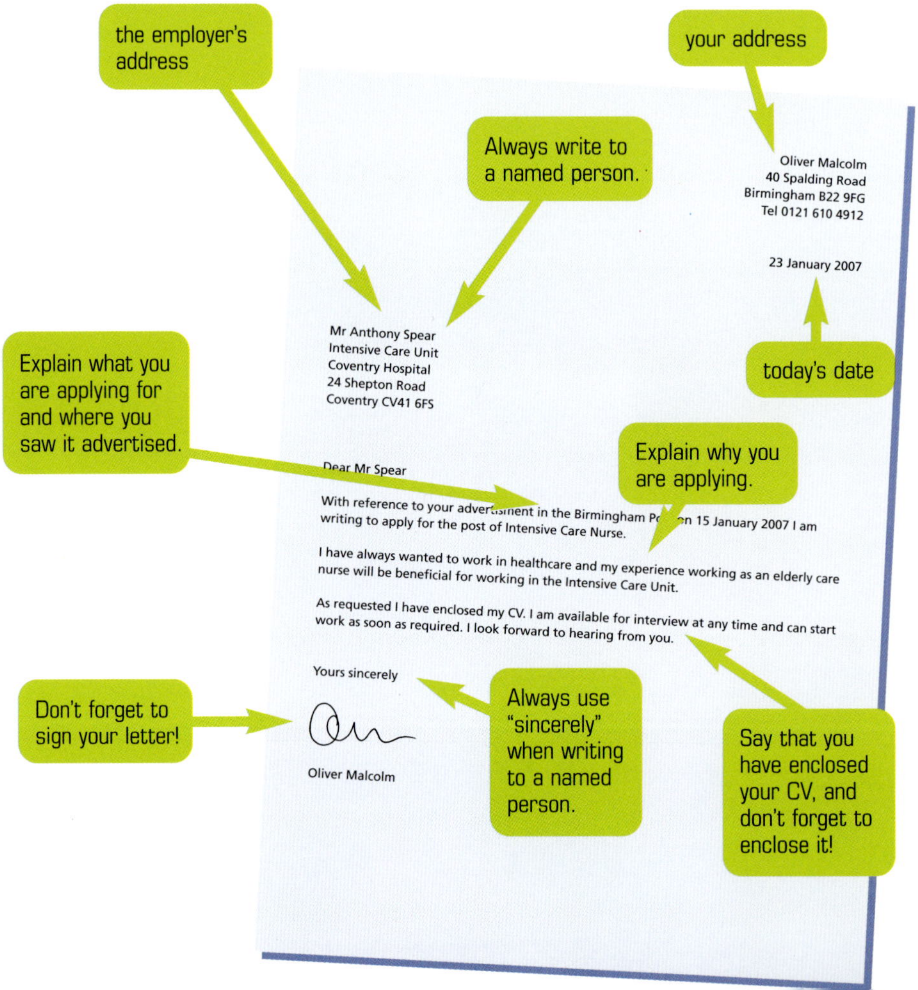

the employer's address
your address
Always write to a named person.
Oliver Malcolm
40 Spalding Road
Birmingham B22 9FG
Tel 0121 610 4912
23 January 2007
Mr Anthony Spear
Intensive Care Unit
Coventry Hospital
24 Shepton Road
Coventry CV41 6FS
today's date
Explain what you are applying for and where you saw it advertised.
Explain why you are applying.
Dear Mr Spear
With reference to your adver ment in the Birmingham P n 15 January 2007 I am writing to apply for the post of Intensive Care Nurse.
I have always wanted to work in healthcare and my experience working as an elderly care nurse will be beneficial for working in the Intensive Care Unit.
As requested I have enclosed my CV. I am available for interview at any time and can start work as soon as required. I look forward to hearing from you.
Yours sincerely
Oliver Malcolm
Don't forget to sign your letter!
Always use "sincerely" when writing to a named person.
Say that you have enclosed your CV, and don't forget to enclose it!

Interviews

Employers interview a lot of people to try and find the best person for the job. You therefore have to show the interviewer that you are that person.

There are a number of things you can do to prepare yourself for an interview. First, find out everything you can about the company and what the job involves. You can then prepare some questions to ask the interviewer about the job – after all, the interview is also an opportunity for you to find out about that particular job and company. You should read through your application form or CV to remind yourself of how you answered any questions. The interviewer is bound to ask you questions related to the information you have given, so be prepared.

On the day of the interview, dress smartly and make sure your appearance is neat and tidy, otherwise an employer will not be impressed. Arrive for the interview 10 minutes early so you will not be worried about being late. In the interview itself the most important thing to do is relax and be yourself. Be enthusiastic and answer all the questions clearly. If you do not understand a question ask the interviewer to explain it, and don't worry if you do not know the answer to a question. Just be honest and do not make things up. Remember to be positive and sell yourself.

INTERVIEW QUESTIONS

Think of answers to these questions before you go for an interview. They are the type of questions interviewers like to ask.

◎ **Why do you want this job?**
◎ **Why do you think you would be good at this job?**
◎ **What are your strengths and weaknesses?**

When the interview is over, it is unlikely that you will find out if you got the job straight away. The company will usually have lots more people to interview before a decision is made. When you do get the result, do not give up if you are unsuccessful – after all, you may have come a close second. Ask the interviewer for feedback. This way you should be able to work out why you didn't get the job and will be able to do better next time.

Chapter 7

Onwards and upwards

Imagine that you have done well at school, obtained all the relevant qualifications, skills, and experience, applied for your ideal job in the healthcare industry, and been successful. Congratulations! So what happens now? How do you shape your career? What opportunities are there for further training and advancement?

Ongoing training while at work

Most employers will provide some form of on-the-job training when you start working for them. Once you are settled in your job there may be further opportunities to train at work, and you should take advantage of these. In order to do well in your chosen career, and hopefully to move onwards and upwards, it is a good idea to get as much training as possible. Some of the types of training offered by employers are described below.

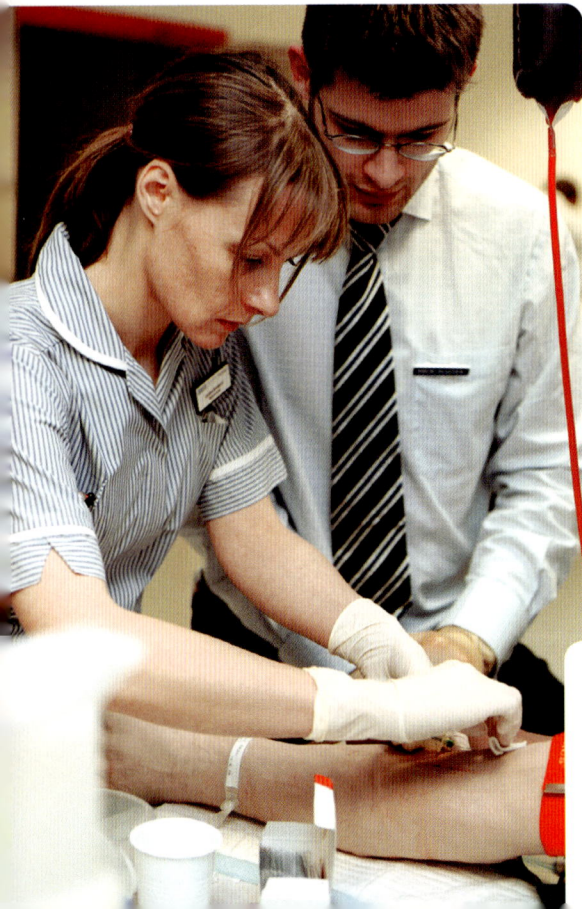

Medical staff

All medical staff are expected to follow continuing medical education throughout their working lives. They are always learning, as new discoveries are made and new technologies continue to develop. They need to keep up to date with any new techniques relevant to their field of medicine and attend courses to improve their skills and knowledge.

left: *On-going training is essential in the healthcare industry.*

Dentists

There is no formal general dental practice career structure, so you can further your knowledge at your own pace and follow the particular dental specialities that are of interest to you. Dentists constantly need to continue to update and further their knowledge and can do so through a wide range of short courses.

Hospital porters

A hospital porter will receive on-the-job training. A large proportion of this training will be in health and safety procedures. This will include how to lift heavy items, how to handle patients, and how to move technical equipment and potentially dangerous medicines.

Where do I go next?

Your prospects for promotion depend on your ability and performance in your job. Many jobs offer the opportunity for promotion to supervisory or managerial levels. There are plenty of opportunities for doctors, nurses, and dentists to work abroad, and in some jobs it is possible to become self-employed.

Doctors and nurses

Once you qualify as a doctor, you can specialize in one of a number of fields. For example, you can become a general practitioner (GP), an anaesthetist, a heart surgeon, or a dermatologist, to name but a few. You will need to undergo further training for most of these specialisms, but once qualified you will be able to achieve consultant status – the top of the medical tree. You could also move into academic work, either carrying out research or teaching medical students.

CASE STUDY

Joseph is a hospital doctor.

The career ladder in medicine is very strictly defined. After graduation you work for a year as a House Officer in a hospital then you progress to the grade of Senior House Officer, where you remain for anything from 2 to 6 years. During this period of time you would ideally try to decide what you want to specialize in and get a job in that specialty. Specialist training schemes vary in length from 4 to 7 years. At the end of specialist training, you are ready to apply for consultant posts.

Promotion opportunities for nurses are good. With experience, you can move up to more senior positions where you will be leading teams of nurses and other staff. You can choose to develop your clinical skills, working with patients, or concentrate on management, teaching, or research.

Dentists, dental nurses, and hygienists

With experience, a dentist can become a partner in a practice or become self-employed and run their own practice. Hospital dentists can specialize in areas such as children's dentistry or dental surgery, and may eventually become consultants. Some dentists study for further postgraduate qualifications, sometimes on a part-time basis. This can lead to dental teaching careers at universities.

below: *All healthcare departments need managers to make sure they run smoothly and efficiently.*

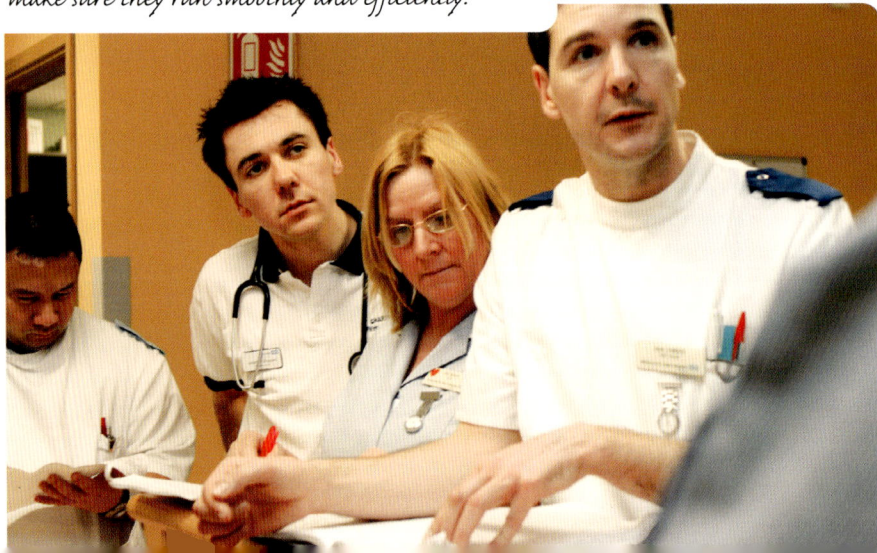

Dental nurses can also go on to specialize in a particular area of dentistry, for example, orthodontic nursing. You could also move into management within your practice or take further qualifications to become a dental hygienist.

Other health professionals

Health professionals, such as physiotherapists, can work their way up through more senior posts to eventually take charge of a department. Paramedics can specialize in driving fast response vehicles or move into training new paramedics. Promotion prospects in radiography are excellent – you could move into a specialist area, such as **ultrasound**, or you could move into management, teaching, or research.

With experience, pharmacists may become self-employed, owning and running their own pharmacies. Pharmacists and pharmacologists may choose to specialize in a particular area of their work, such as preparing medicines, or move into research, management, or teaching roles.

Transferable skills

People who succeed in the healthcare industry develop a range of people and communication skills that can also be useful in other jobs. Within the industry there are plenty of opportunities at all levels for you to create an interesting career for yourself. However, for some there may come a time when you feel the need to move out of the industry, and these so-called **transferable skills** will enable you to do that.

WORKING ABROAD

There are good opportunities for doctors, nurses, dentists, and radiographers to work abroad. There are many reasons for healthcare professionals wanting to work abroad, ranging from wanting a break from the NHS, to the desire to experience another culture. Here are a few examples of some of the organizations you can contact for further information:

◎ Medicins Sans Frontieres (http://www.msf.org/unitedkingdom/)

◎ British Red Cross Overseas (http://www.redcross.org.uk/section. asp?id=39997)

◎ Expedition Medical Training (http://www.voyageconcepts.co.uk/ expemed.htm)

Chapter 8

Conclusion

So, are you still interested in pursuing a career in healthcare? The industry can certainly offer you a challenging and varied career, with plenty of opportunities for promotion. You will have to work hard to get there though, as a lot of people see healthcare as a rewarding industry to work in. Many people also think that working in this area will only involve caring for sick people. You know better than that! You know that for many jobs in healthcare you will be working in a laboratory, not with patients. You know that the hours you work are likely to be long and that you will have to do a lot of training before you qualify for more specialist jobs. You also know that you will have to work some evenings and weekends, when you would much rather be out having a good time with your friends.

Making the right choice

You need to think very carefully about what you want from your career. Different people want different things, and the sooner you decide what you want to do, the sooner you can start working towards gaining the relevant qualifications.

below: *Want to work in healthcare? Start now by going on a first aid course.*

You also need to decide if you are the right person to enjoy working in the healthcare industry. It is certainly not for everyone. As competition for jobs is likely to be strong you need to have the right personality and the right skills, as well as the right qualifications. You also need to have some work experience, particularly of working with people. Once you have all this under your belt you will be well placed for applying for a job in the healthcare industry. Then all you need to do is stand out from the crowd. Good luck!

Jobs in healthcare

- Ambulance care assistant
- Ambulance driver
- Anaesthetist
- Chemist
- Children's nurse
- Clinical scientist
- Counsellor
- Dental hygienist
- Dental surgeon
- Dental nurse
- Dental technician
- Dentist
- Dermatologist
- District nurse
- Elderly care nurse
- GP
- Health promotion officer
- Hospital administrator
- Hospital doctor
- Hospital porter
- Immunologist
- Intensive care nurse
- Lab technician
- Locum doctor
- Medical scientist
- Mental health nurse
- Microbiologist
- Midwife
- Neurologist
- Occupational therapist
- Ophthalmic nurse
- Optician
- Optometrist
- Paediatrician
- Pain relief nurse
- Paramedic
- Pharmacist
- Pharmacologist
- Physiotherapist
- Psychiatrist
- Radiographer
- Radiologist
- Social worker
- Speech therapist
- Surgeon
- Virologist

Please note that qualifications and courses are subject to change.

Publications

◎ Fields, Jennifer. *World of Work: Choosing a Career as a Nurse-Midwife* (Rosen, 2001)

◎ Malladi, Niriksha. *So You Want to Be a Doctor?* (Frederick Fell, 2005)

◎ McAlpine, Margaret. *So You Want to Work in Healthcare* ` (Hodder Wayland, 2004)

◎ Vallano, Annette. *Your Career in Nursing: Manage Your Future in the Changing World of Healthcare* (Kaplan, 2003)

Careers websites

◎ City and Guilds (www.city-and-guilds.co.uk)
   – This website tells you all about City and Guilds qualifications.

◎ Connexions Direct (www.connexions-direct.com)
   – This website gives advice to young people, including learning and careers. Includes link to the Jobs4U careers database.

◎ Learndirect (www.learndirect-advice.co.uk) and Learndirect Scotland (www.learndirectscotland.com/)
   – Go to "job profiles" for details of many jobs in healthcare and courses and qualifications.

◎ Modern Apprenticeships, Scotland (www.scottish-enterprise.com/modernapprenticeships)
   – Check out the case studies of people already training.

◎ Need2Know: Learning (www.need2know.co.uk/learning)
   – This site gives you information about study and qualifications.

◎ Qualifications and Curriculum Authority (www.qca.org.uk/14-19)
   – go to "Qualifications" and click on "Main qualification groups" to find out about NVQs.

◎ Scottish Vocational Qualifications (www.sqa.org.uk)
   – You can find out all the latest qualifications information here.

◎ The National Council for Work Experience (www.work-experience.org/)
   – Go to "Students and Graduates" to search for placements.

Get ahead in healthcare!

The following organizations may be able to provide further information.

◎ British Association of Dental Nurses (www.badn.org.uk)
   – Got to this website for nursing news and course updates.

◎ British Dental Association (www.bda-dentistry.org.uk)
   – Look at "BDA 3D Mouth", the educational section of the BDA's website, which has advice on dental health and hygiene.

◎ British Medical Association (www.bma.org.uk)
   – The BMA is the professional association for doctors.

◎ British Society for Clinical Neurophysiology (www.bscn.org.uk)
   – Go to the careers section to read how several trainees got into neurophysiology and what they do in their day-to-day work.

◎ Chartered Society of Physiotherapy (www.csp.org.uk)
   – This website covers everything about physiotherapy, from careers to issues in the workplace, to clinical guidelines.

◎ General Medical Council (www.gmc-uk.org)
   – Go to "Education" to learn about training and courses

◎ Institute of Biomedical Science (www.ibms.org)
   – See "Education and Careers" for details of courses.

◎ Nursing and Midwifery Council (www2.nmc4jobs.com)
   – Go to "Find an Employer" to look at current job vacancies

◎ Royal Pharmaceutical Society of Great Britain (www.rpsgb.org.uk)
   – Find out about pharmacists and pharmacy on this website.

◎ Society of Radiographers (www.sor.org)
   – To find out more about a career in radiography, click on the link on the home page.

◎ The Royal College of Psychiatry (www.rcpsych.ac.uk)
   – You will find lots of information here about mental health, examinations, training, and careers in psychiatry.

Glossary

accreditation official approval or recognition

anaesthetist specialist doctor who uses drugs to put a patient to sleep before an operation

apprenticeship training scheme that allows you to work for money, learn, and become qualified at the same time

bereavement feelings of loss because someone close to you has died

consultant person who has a lot of experience and provides expert professional advice

counselling listening to people's problems and giving them support

depression feeling of sadness that makes you think there is no hope

dermatologist doctor who treats skin problems

distance learning method of studying where lessons are broadcast on television or over the Internet

dosage amount of medicine that you should take at a time

General Medical Council (GMC) regulator of the medical profession in the UK

general practitioner (GP) doctor who works in the community as a family doctor

immune system system of organs and processes in the body that provides protectection from infection and disease

immunologist scientist who studies how the body reacts to diseases and how to prevent diseases

intensive care department in a hospital that gives special care to patients who are dangerously ill

interpret explain the meaning of something

locum doctor who provides cover for another doctor who is ill or on holiday

meningitis disease that affects the brain, caused by infection

micro-organism tiny organism that causes disease

midwife special type of nurse who provides care and advice to pregnant women and their families

motor neurone disease disease that causes a gradual loss of control of the muscles and nerves in the body

National Health Service (NHS) organization that provides all kinds of healthcare for everyone in the UK

National Vocational Qualification (NVQ) in England and Wales, a work-related, competence-based qualification that shows you have the knowledge and skills to do a job effectively. NVQs represent national standards that are recognized by employers throughout the UK.

on call be prepared to work if you are needed

optician person who tests people's eyes and prescribes glasses and contact lenses

paramedic person who is trained to give emergency first aid to people who are injured

persistence continuing to do something even though it is difficult

pharmacist person who is trained to prepare medicines

pharmacy shop where medicines are sold; also, the study of medicine

post-natal depression illness where a woman feels sad after her baby is born

prescribe advise and give permission to a patient to use a medicine

physiotherapist person who treats problems caused by injuries to muscles, nerves, and bones, to help people regain physical fitness and mobility

promotion move to a more important job in an organization

radiographer person who uses X-ray machines to look inside the human body

refer send someone to a medical specialist for treatment

referee person willing to testify in writing about the character or ability of a job applicant

sandwich course university or college course that includes a period of time spent working in industry

schizophrenia mental illness where someone hears or feels things that are not real

Scottish Vocational Qualification (SVQ) in Scotland, a work-related, competence-based qualification that shows you have the knowledge and skills to do a job effectively. SVQs represent national standards that are recognized by employers throughout the UK.

statistics numbers that represent facts

sterilize make something completely clean

stroke sudden attack caused by an interruption to the flow of blood in the brain

tolerance allow people to do or say what they want without judging them

transferable skills skills that you have learnt at school or in a job that can be used in another job

ultrasound medical technique that produces an image of something inside your body

vaccine substance that is used to protect people from disease

virus tiny living thing that causes disease

work shadowing following a more senior employee at work to find out what their job involves

Index

Titles in the *How to get ahead in* series include:

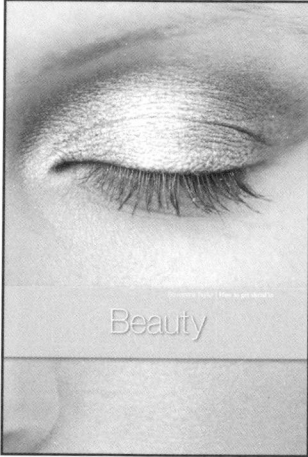

Hardback 978 1 4062 0442 1

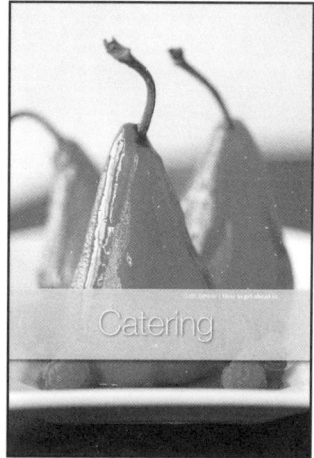

Hardback 978 1 4062 0443 8

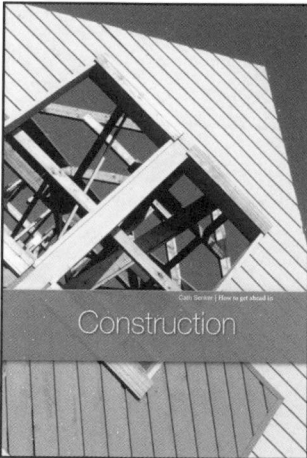

Hardback 978 1 4062 0440 7

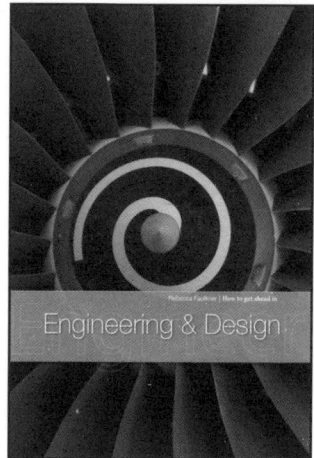

Hardback 978 1 4062 0441 4

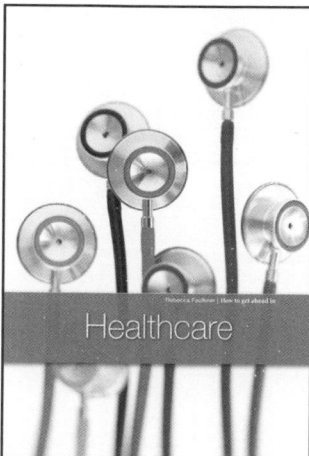

Hardback 978 1 4062 0444 5

Other titles available:

Armed and Civilian Forces	Hardback 978 1 4062 0450 6
Finance	Hardback 978 1 4062 0448 3
IT and Administration	Hardback 978 1 4062 0449 0
Leisure and Tourism	Hardback 978 1 4062 0447 6
Retail	Hardback 978 1 4062 0446 9

Find out about the other titles in this series on our website at www.raintreepublishers.co.uk

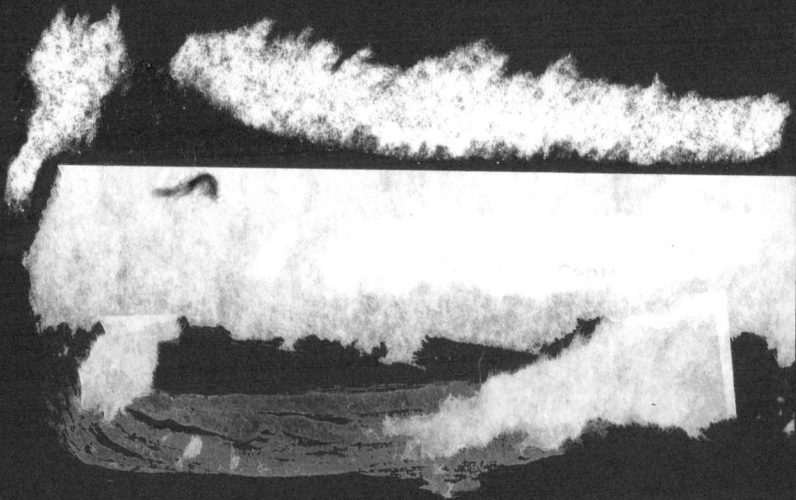